D0769307

THE DRINK-SPOTTY BOOK

THE
DRINK-SPOTTY
BOOK

PELHAM WITHERSPOON

ILLUSTRATED BY

ffolkes & *HEATH*

BANTAM PRESS
NEW YORK · LONDON · TORONTO · SYDNEY · AUCKLAND

TRANSWORLD PUBLISHERS LTD
Century House
61–63 Uxbridge Road
London W5 5SA

TRANSWORLD PUBLISHERS (AUSTRALIA) PTY LTD
26 Harley Crescent
Condell Park
NSW 2200

TRANSWORLD PUBLISHERS (NZ) LTD
Cnr. Moselle & Waipareira Aves,
Henderson
Auckland

Published 1985 by Bantam Press,
a division of Transworld Publishers Ltd

British Library Cataloguing in Publication Data

Witherspoon, Pelham
　　Drink-spotties.
　　I. Title
　　823′.91409　　　PR6073.18/

　　ISBN 0-593-01007-8

　　Printed in West Germany by
　　Mohndruck Graphische Betriebe GmbH, Gütersloh

DEDICATION

—— ✳ ——

This book is dedicated to
Peter Stuart Allenby Edwards
and to my dear mother, both of whom have been
of immense inspiration in its creation.

—— ✳ ——

ACKNOWLEDGEMENTS

———— ✳ ————

I acknowledge with very great thanks, the various help and contributions which I have received from: Claire Sandford, who gave up so much of her spare time to typing the script; Kerry Hood, without whose encouragement the book would never have been written; Patrick Janson-Smith, my indefatigable Publisher; Nicholas Case, Mardie Morris-Jones, Rachel Vincent, Philippa McFarlane, Gilly Stewart, and, above all, Miriam Mead for all their suggestions; and, of course, my two dedicatees.

Preface

To the uninitiated, a Drinks Party (properly pronounced DRINK-SPOTTY) can be a disconcerting experience. It is defined in this book as 'an ingenious way of returning hospitality by getting as many people as possible to stand in a room and make a lot of noise'. That is exactly what it is. If you are unfamiliar with this particular social habit you will find it an unnerving business.

Not only will you be forced to squeeze into an extremely crowded room, and shout to make yourself heard, but you will also need to adapt to a wholly new language. This is where *THE DRINK-SPOTTY BOOK* can help you. Carry it with you, and you will be guided through a minefield of potentially unintelligible social intercourse.

But first a bit of background. A DRINK-SPOTTY is a peculiarly English institution, though it owes its origin to the American habit of serving cocktails. Some years ago one had cocktail parties, but since the art of making cocktails has lapsed one now has DRINK-SPOTTIES. The idea is the same, however: to foregather before lunch or dinner for an aperitif or three. It is also a convenient method of repaying hospitality in bulk. You just invite dozens of people you would prefer not to have to put up with individually and pack them into a room together and let them get on with it.

Although there are many different types of DRINK-SPOTTY (smart London, bohemian, country weekend, institutional etc), the following is an approximation, for the benefit of the unfamiliar, of a standard London DRINK-SPOTTY, held on a mid-week evening.

You will have been invited, by means of a card bearing the words AT HAME, for 7.30 p.m. Some years ago, this would have been 6.30 p.m. but DRINK-SPOTTIES now tend to begin one hour later. Despite this inexplicable postponement, you should nevertheless (if you are male) arrive in your work uniform (stripes and spots suggested), even if this involves sitting at home for a good hour or so, all trussed up and feeling uncomfortable. This is not out of any sense of deference to your hostess, but merely to demonstrate that you are the sort of person who goes to work in uniform. The only possible change of clothing will be your socks – to change from a relatively sober pair to a bright red or yellow pair – in order to show that you are capable of appearing decent.

Although the time is specified, you should arrive about half an hour (HAR PHNAR) late so that you can make an entrance. When you do arrive, you will find that it is imperative to make a lot of noise. Experienced DRINK-SPOTTY goers always make a lot of noise – when they arrive, while they are there and when they leave. It is also imperative upon arrival to kiss every girl you meet. If you are a girl then you must kiss girls and boys. It is compulsory not only to plant a kiss on both sides of the recipient's face but also, while doing so, to make the sound MWAH! This can be followed by a variety of expressions, the most usual of which is 'LARV-LID-SEE-YOUR'. It is part of the fun of DRINK-SPOTTIES that you will be kissing people whom you would never dream of kissing at any other time of the day or on any other occasion.

You will then encounter the problem of introductions. It is extremely bad form to make an intelligible introduction. You will find that your hostess will say to a third party 'Do you know ———'; your own name will have disappeared in a garbled blur, and the third party will say HIGH JI-DOUR without having registered a single syllable of it. The third party may then conceivably say WATCH-UDOUR. This will be an enquiry as to what you do for a living and you will embark in all sincerity on an attempted explanation, only to realize that you could have done with a megaphone and an ear-trumpet. After a feeble attempt at answering the question, you will probably find the third party much more interested in something else. He or she will either be looking over your shoulder at someone who has just walked in the room or will have actually moved away to start shouting at someone else. You should not take this as necessarily meaning that your job sounds terribly dull, but rather that he or she was never terribly interested in meeting you in the first place.

Apart from talking about jobs, conversation will to some extent be governed by the time of year. Early in the New Year you will be asked whether you have any skiing plans; in February and March it will be a question of where you have been skiing. In the spring you will be asked about summer holiday plans and which weddings you are going to, and, later in the summer, where you have been. In the autumn it will be plans for Christmas and so on. Such is the nature of DRINK-SPOTTY conversation that you will probably not get more than a vague response, such as AIR-RALLY, since the other person will have launched into a long discourse on his or her own plans. Whatever happens, you should not expect a lot in the way of intellectual stimulus.

Occasionally, however, you will meet someone whose company you quite enjoy and with whom, despite the lack of megaphones etc, you have quite fruitful discussion. It will be at that very moment that your hostess will forcibly separate you from that person and impose you, quite against your will, on another person who is also in the middle of a conversation, whom you have no desire to meet. The process of introductions and riveting discussion will then start all over again. You will pass a couple of boisterous hours engaged in this way, being fed from time to time with a glass of wine or whatever. You may also be given a carrot; the idea is to bite the end off it, having first stuck it into the accompanying sauce.

It will then be time to leave.

Departures are similar to arrivals in that maximum noise is made, especially in the road outside, and maximum slamming of car doors. The kissing process is repeated with even more MWAH's. One of the most popular parting remarks is MUZD'V-LUNGE. This does not mean that it is lunchtime. In fact it is a deliberate trick; it means that you have no intention of having lunch at any time with the person to whom you have just said it. An alternative is MUZGIBBIN-TUDGE. Likewise, this means that neither party has any desire to see the other again.

Be sure to make a hasty getaway, to avoid getting press-ganged into going to an even noisier and more crowded place for a late supper, where you will almost certainly end up paying for the person next to you, whom you have never met before, and whom you are not mad about seeing again.

Instead, you should slope off home gratefully, with stiff legs and back, a splitting headache and chronically hoarse of voice, having thoroughly enjoyed your evening.

If, having read this Preface, you are totally bemused: do not worry. You must now study carefully the following pages, so that, at the very least, you master the rudiments of acceptable DRINK-SPOTTY terminology.

Good Luck!

P.W.
London, 1985

THE DRINK-SPOTTY BOOK

ABITE   *Approximately; but see* **ARIND**

AIRHELLAIR   *A casual form of greeting. See* **HELLAIR**

AIRMPLEFOTH   *A public school in NW England*

AIRNAIR   *An expression of dismay, or incredulity*

AIR-RALLY

A suitably blasé response to a scintillating remark

AIR-RALLY	*A suitably blasé response to a scintillating remark*
AIRSCUT	*Well-known* RACE-COSS *in* BOCKSHAH
AIVERCHAW	*An opening or introduction; can be a musical work*
AIX	*A famous horse-race, which takes place on* EPSOM DINES, *on the Saturday after the* DOBBY
AMRAL COD	*A famous* PUBLIC HICE *in London*
ANDERLAPE	*A famous* PUBLIC HICE *in London*
AP-SLOOTLEH	*An earnest and emphatic, though usually insincere, adverb*

ARIND

This is similar in meaning to ABITE, *and often used together:* ARIND-NER-BITE

ARLAND

The large island to the west of Wales. See NORN ARLAND

ARM

A reflective pause, or hesitation, mid-sentence

ASIAN

With a soft 's' this means a large area of sea, as in 'TLAIRNTIC *or* P'CIVIC; *with a hard 's' it means a* CHAIRP *from the* CONT'NENT *of Asia, as in* 'YER EVRIDGE JOHNNY BAMESE'

AXSHLEH

This is a word used at the end of a sentence by way of explanation, as in 'I LIVE IN CITHE-KEN AXSHLEH'

AYB'N | A small place on the west KAIST of Scotland, famous for the AYB'N Ball

AYTELL | A HICE or inn providing accommodation

AYVAL, THE | A famous KRIGGIT GRIND in CITHE London

BAILER
A type of HAIRT *sometimes still worn in* THE SIDDEH

BAIRD
OP-SIT *of* GOURD

BAIRGS
Luggage; is also occasionally used to describe TRYZERS

BAITER
A type of HAIRT *worn at* KIZE *or* HENLAIR

BAMA	*Country in Asia, whose natives are called* **BAMESE.** *See* ASIAN
BAY-TRACE	*Famous annual* RAING *event between Putney and Mortlake*
BEARER-STAH	*See* LOI'R
BEARNAISE	*(a) A type of sauce which can accompany beef;* *(b) as in* 'BEARNAISE CHAIRP 'MPAWMERE WISKIN-SADER'
BENKAH	*Someone in the banking business, as in* MUCHAN BENKAH
BESTER	*See* BRIDDESH
BILES	*One's insides*
BLARD	*The stuff that runs through the veins (alleged to be blue). See* EGGAN

BOCKSHAH	*A* KINETEH *to the west of London*
BRAICH	*See* JERL-REH
BRAIRNDEH	*A type of burnt* WAH-IN *usually drunk after dinner*
BRASHER	*A sort of explanatory leaflet*
BRIDDESH	*Adjective describing a native of* BRIDD'N. *It can also, when preceded by* BESTER, *be an expression of good luck*
BRIDD'N	*One's nation*
BRIGGER-DAH	*An officer in the* OMMEH, *an inordinate number of whom seem to have* RETARD *and to be living in* KEMBLEH *or* HOTLEY-WINTNEH

BRIGGER-DAH

An officer in the OMMEH, *an inordinate number of whom seem to have* RETARD *and to be living in* KEMBLEH *or* HOTLY-WINTNEH

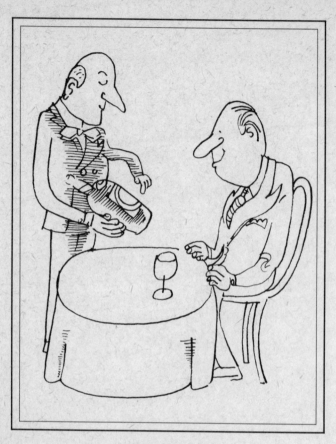

BUGGANDEH

A type of WAH-IN *from SE Central* FRONCE

BRINEBRAIGS	*A gentleman's brown walking shoes*
BUCK'NM-SHAH	*A* KINETEH *NW of London*
BUDDENHELL	*A single bloom worn in one's lapel*
BUGGANDEH	*A type of* WAH-IN *from SE Central* FRONCE
BUNCHER	*See* FLAHZ
BURBRUH	*If one wears a* MEGGINTOSH *this is probably what one would wear*

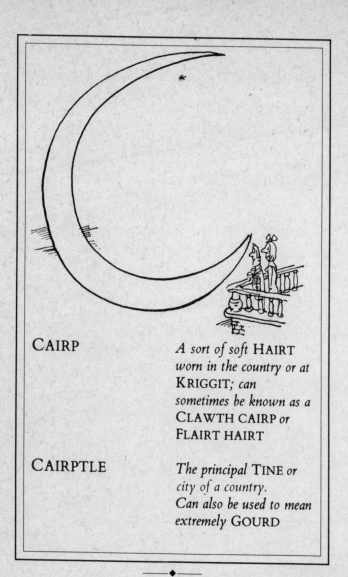

CAIRP

A sort of soft HAIRT worn in the country or at KRIGGIT; can sometimes be known as a CLAWTH CAIRP or FLAIRT HAIRT

CAIRPTLE

The principal TINE or city of a country. Can also be used to mean extremely GOURD

CARE-LINE	*A* GEL's *name*
CAT-TRAINER	*A* GEL's *name*
CHAIRP	*A* CLAIK-YAL *way of describing another male. The word* FELLAY *can also be used. The word* MAIRN, *however, is normally reserved for a servant, or other rank; but see* ELL-MAIRN
CHELT'NUM	*A* TINE *in* GLAWST-SHAH, *famous for* RACIN, *particularly the* CHEMP-Y'N-HUDDLE
CHESTER-DRAWZ	*An article of* FUNNY-CHAH *in one's bedroom for keeping* CLAITHES *in*
CHODDERED KINE-TENT	*A manipulator of monetary matters*
CHODDERED SVAIR	*A professional adviser on property matters*

CLARB

An institution or society of recreation, relaxation or fellowship of varying nature. There are many of these in PELL MELL *and* SN'JEMZIZ. *Every* CHAIRP *must have one*

◆

CHOLLS	*A* CHAIRP's *name*
CHOMMIN	*A complimentary adjective*
CHOMMINGEL	*A complimentary way of describing a* GEL
CHOOB	CLAIK-YAL *term for the* UND'GRIND
CHOOLDREN	*Offspring or issue*
CHPAIRN	*Country in NE Asia*
CHUDDERHICE	*A public school in Surrey (whose Old Boys'* KRIGGIT *team is called the* FRAHZ)
CHUR	*A thing you sit on*
CHURZ	*A somewhat vulgar farewell or toast. See* RIND
CHUTCH	*A building used for religious service*

CHUTCHELL | *Extremely well-known* BRIDDESH P'LIDDIGLE *figure*

CITHE | *Point of the compass* OP-SIT *to* NOTH, *as in* CITHE-KEN, *an area of London*

CLAIK-YAL | *Appertaining to common speech or* ORNREH *conversation*

CLAIN-YAL | *Appertaining to the Colonies*

CLAITHES | *Wearing apparel. See* WAR-DRABE

CLARB | *An institution or society of recreation, relaxation or fellowship of varying nature. There are many of these in* PELL MELL *and* SN'JEMZIZ. *Every* CHAIRP *must have one*

CRAIKIE

A leisurely game played on a lawn, using mallets, balls and hoops

CLARNT	One who takes advice from a SLIZDAH or CHODDERED KINE-TENT
CLAWTH	See CAIRP
CLEARIT	Red table WAH-IN from Bordeaux region of FRONCE
CLUMBAY	The CAIRPTLE of SLON
C'MELLAH	A GEL's name
CONT'NENT	A large land mass; see EARFRIGGER, MERRIGGER, YORUP, etc. This word is often used to describe the land the other side of the English Channel
COPPRIT F'NAIRNCE	The sort of job that some of the CHAIRPS have in THE SIDDEH

CRAIKIE	*A leisurely game played on a lawn, using mallets, balls and hoops*
CR'VAIRT	*A piece of silk occasionally worn round the neck, not unlike a* SCOFF
CRYDE	*A lot of people, usually fairly* TARSUM. *You will find one of these at nearly every* DRINK-SPOTTY
CRY-DID	*Adjective of* CRYDE

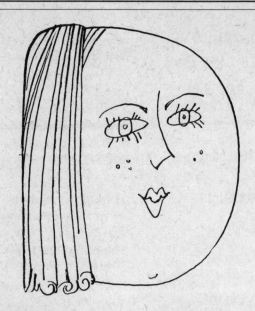

DAH-MANS   *See* JERL-REH

DAINCHER NAY   *A rhetorical enquiry, always at the end of a sentence*

DAR-RARE   *Looseness of* BILES *(but see* VUBBLE-DAR-RARE)

DEMPRIDDIEGEL	*A complimentary way of describing a* GEL
DERBISSER	*See* STCHOPPID
DINE	OP-SIT *of* UP
DIVI-GUL	OP-SIT *of easy*
DIZZEN	*An adjective meaning acceptable, amenable or pleasant as in* 'VEDDEH DIZZEN-VIEW, ELL-MAIRN'
DIZZER-GRAIRBLE	*Unpleasant, unco-opera-tive or* TARSUM
D'MYNIFFER-DOO	*A suitably reticent expression of consent, usually in terms of accepting a drink. See* RIND

DEMPRIDDIEGEL

A complimentary way of describing a GEL

DOBBY

*A very well-known
annual horse-race, held
on* EPSOM DINES

DRINK-SPOTTY

*An ingenious way of
returning hospitality by
getting as many people as
possible to stand in a
room and make a lot of
noise*

D'YARAY-D'YAH

*A term of mild regret or
of slightly amused
surprise*

EARCHIFF MUSSHLE *The most senior rank in the* ROLL EARFOSS

EARCROFT *The singular and plural of an aeroplane*

EARFRIGGER *The* CONT'NENT *to the* CITHE *of the* MED'TRAINYAN

EARLENBEH	*First World War general*
EARLICK- ZONDER	*Second World War general*
EARNDROO	*A CHAIRP's name*
EDEN-'MBELL-Y'L	*A pretty DIZZEN education*
EGGAN-BLARD	*The name given to the bilious-looking tie worn at LODD'S*
ELDER RAVIAN	*Old Boy of public school in NW London*
ELDY TAINYAN	*Old Boy of public school near Windsor, BOCKSHAH*
ELL-MAIRN	*An affectionate way of addressing another CHAIRP regardless of his age*

EARCROFT

The singular and plural of an aeroplane

ELL-TRAIRF'D	*A famous KRIGGIT GRIND in LAIRNK-SHAH (the football bit isn't usually referred to)*
EMBRUH	*The CAIRPTLE of Scotland*
EMPAH	*That marvellous institution and era when BRIDD'N almost ruled the world*
EM'SEH	*The official residence of an 'MBAIRSTER*
EPSOM DINES	*See DOBBY*
EVRIDGE	*Medium or mean*

FAWTHFASTWAW *The period of time before 1914*

FAWTHWAW *The period of time before 1939*

F'DOGRAFEH *The art of taking* **FAYDERGROFFS** *(which are sometimes known as* **SNAIRPS***)*

FEARZZANT	*A type of* GEM *bird*
FELLAY	*See* CHAIRP *and* M'DAHFELLAY
FEMMLEH POTTRITS	*Term used to describe paintings of revered and long-deceased ancestors*
FILL MUSSHLE	*The most senior rank in the* OMMEH
FILLY-BINS	*A group of islands in the* CITHE *China Sea*
FLAHZ	*Things that* CHAIRPS *give* GELS *(usually in a* BUNCHER*)*
FLAIRT	*(a) one's place in* TINE *(b) the type of* RACIN *where the* NAIRGS *do not jump over the sticks. Famous examples of* FLAIRT RACIN *are the* TOOTH-IZIN GINNEARS, *the*

DOBBY *and the* AIX. *Examples of the other type of* RACIN, *where they do jump, are the* GREN-NESH'NL *and the* GELD-CUP *and the* CHEMP-Y'N-HUDDLE *at* CHELT'NUM

FLURRED — *Rather nasty type of* TRYZERS *which have widened bottoms*

FORDYARZERGAIR — *Very approximately 40 years previously*

FRAHZ — *See* CHUDDERHICE

FRAWST — *State of freezing*

FRIGGIT — *A type of ship used by the* ROLL NEVVEH

FRONCE — *A country situated in* YORUP

FEMMLEH POTTRITS

*Term used to describe paintings of revered and
long-deceased ancestors*

FUNNY-CHAH   *That which is sat upon (as in CHUR and SAFER), as well as that which one puts drinks on or CLAITHES in (such as CHESTER-DRAWZ and WAR-DRABE)*

F'DOGRAFEH

The art of taking FAYDERGROFFS (which are sometimes known as SNAIRPS)

◆

49

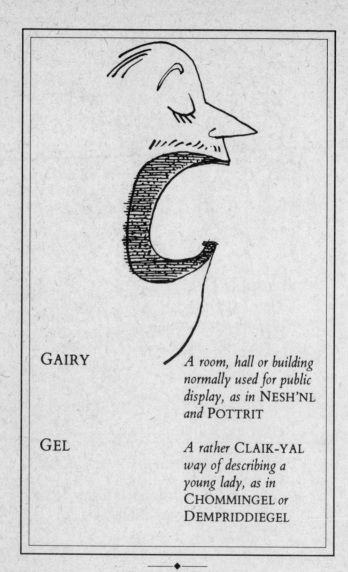

GAIRY　　　　　　*A room, hall or building normally used for public display, as in* NESH'NL *and* POTTRIT

GEL　　　　　　　*A rather* CLAIK-YAL *way of describing a young lady, as in* CHOMMINGEL *or* DEMPRIDDIEGEL

GELD	*See* JERL-REH
GELD-CUP	*A famous horse-race.. See* FLAIRT *– although it isn't*
GEM	*This is not to be confused with* GEMZ; *rather, it is the name given to the creatures which one shoots, such as* FEARZZANT, GRICE *and* POTTRICH
GEMZ	*These are not to be confused with* GEM *or* SPOT; *rather, they are recreational activities, such as* CRAIKIE, KRIGGIT, PAYLAY, SQUORSH *and* THLEDDIX
GERMY	*A* CHAIRP's *name*
GLARZGAY	*Sort of place you have to go through to get to the* AYB'N *Ball*

GAIRY

A room, hall or building normally used for public display, as in NESH'NL *and* POTTRIT

GLAWST-SHAH	*A* KINETEH DINE *the end of the M4, ideal for spending weekends in*
GODDEN POTTY	*A* SAYSHLE *gathering in the* GRINDS *of a* HICE
GODS	*Well-known Brigade in the* OMMEH
GOFF	*A* GEM *played with a small white ball. It should never be pronounced 'goalf'*
GORN	*Past participle of the verb 'to go'*
GOSSLEH	*An adjective similar in meaning to 'awful' or 'frightful'. It is frequently preceded by* SEMPLEH
GOURD	OP-SIT *of* BAIRD

GRAVE-NAH	*An extensive estate in London*
GREN-NESH'NL	*A very famous horse-race. See* FLAIRT *– although it isn't*
GRICE	*A bird shot on* MAWS *between August and November*
GRIND	*A sward on which* KRIGGIT *is played*
GRINDS	*The area of ornamentally cultivated land surrounding a* HICE
GUMMENT	*The governing body in a state*
GUMMENT HICE	*The official residence of the Governor of a Colony*

GOSSLEH

An adjective similar in meaning to 'awful' or
'frightful'.

HAIR-BER-DAIR-SHER ZAIRSX *A public school in* HALF-A-SHAH

HAIRNGAJIFF *or* POGGIT HAIRNGAJIFF, *which is a piece of silk protruding from one's breast* POGGIT

HAIRNTS	A KINETEH *SW of London*
HAIRT	*Collective noun for types of headgear*
HAIRY	*A CHAIRP's name*
HALF-A-SHAH	*A KINETEH to the NOTH of London*
HAME, AT	*The location of a DRINK-SPOTTY*
HARBOUR-CHEW	*An enquiry as to how the other person is, or what he would like to drink. See RIND*
HAR PHNAR	*Approximately 30 minutes*
HAYB'N	*Part of London famous for its VARDUCT*
HELEBRUH	*A public school in HALF-A-SHAH*

HELLAIR	*A casual form of greeting, less formal than* HIGH JI-DOUR *but not as casual as* AIRHELLAIR. *It is frequently followed immediately by* HIGH YOUR
HENLAIR	*A* TINE *upon the River Thames famous for its* RIGGEARTAH *and* RAING
HERRA-GIT	*A very solid spa* TINE *in* YOCKSHAH
HICE	*A type of residence*
HICEHELD KEVELRAIR	*Well-known* OMMEH *Regiment*
HIGH JI-DOUR	*A rather formal manner of greeting*
HIGH-SPOTTY	*A weekend in the country when you stay with someone else*

HAIRT

Collective noun for types of headgear

HIGH YOUR	*A vague enquiry as to someone's health. As with* HIGH JI-DOUR, *this is never answered*
H'MARLYERS	*A range of very high mountains to the* NOTH *of* INJURE
HOLLY STRIT	*A part of London well known for the practice of* MEDSUN
HOT SOJURN	*A type of doctor often found in* HOLLY STRIT
HOTLY-WINTNEH	*A* TINE *in* HAIRNTS *famous for* RETARD BRIGGER-DAHS
HUDDLE	*See* CHELT'NUM
H'YOO-GAY	*A* CHAIRP'*s name*

HIGH JI-DOUR

A rather formal manner of greeting

IDD'LEH
A Latin country, whose
natives are TEARLIANS

INE-DLE
A public school in Rutland

INJURE
Sub-CONT'NENT of
Asia, formerly the Jewel
of the EMPAH, which
used to have a very fine
OMMEH called the
INJURE NOMMEH

INNENITE	*A well-known* CLARB, *in* PIGGERDILLAIR
ITE	*The* OP-SIT *of in. In* KRIGGIT, *it means being dismissed*
ITE-HICE	*A stable or barn, or place you store your logs*
IZIN	*A word used to describe (in the first person) previous presence, as in* 'IZIN INJURE FAWTHWAW, THEN IZIN THE SIDDEH, NARM RETARD.' IZIN *in this sense should not be confused with either the famous* KRIGGIT CLARB, IZIN-GARI, *or the famous* FLAIRT *race, the* TOOTH-IZIN GINNEARS

JAH-ILLS   *A* CHAIRP's *name*

JAIRKIT   *Apart from a* DINNER
                 JAIRKIT *and a* SMAKIN
                 JAIRKIT *it should be
                 remembered that
                 'gentlemen wear*
                 KATES; *potatoes wear*
                 JAIRKITS'

JAIRPS	*Natives of* CHPAIRN
JEAN-TEA	*A very popular drink, consisting of ice, lemon, tonic water and gin*
JERL-REH	*Articles of personal adornment. All* GELS *have* JERL-REH *of course, but do not* ORFEN *mention it.* BRAICHES *and* PARLS *will be seen at all* DRINK-SPOTTIES, *as well as* GELD *and* DAH-MANS. *The most famous collection of* JERL-REH *is at the* TAH *of London: the* KRINE-JOOLS
JOOLYAH	*A* GEL's *name*
JUKE	*A title of nobility ranking next below that of a Prince*

JUKER BOOT	*A famous* PUBLIC HICE *in London*
JUMNS	*Natives of* JUMNY
JUMNY	*A country situated in* YORUP
JUZZEH	*A woollen over-garment*

JERL-REH

Articles of personal adornment. All GELS *have*
JERL-REH *of course, but do not* ORFEN *mention it.*
BRAICHES *and* PARLS *will be seen at all* DRINK-
SPOTTIES, *as well as* GELD *and* DAH-MANS

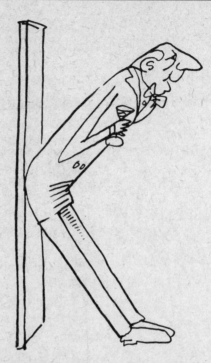

KAIRTCHAKAIRB *A verb meaning to hire a taxi; likewise* HAILER-HAIRNSM

KAIST *The side of the land next to the sea*

KATE	*An over-garment. See* JAIRKIT
KEMBLEH	*A* TINE *in Surrey famous for its* OMMEH *connection*
KEMBRIDGE	*A famous* VOSSTEH, *city and* KINETEH *in East Anglia*
KEVELRAIR	*Horse* SELL-JAHS. *See* HICEHELD
KINETEH	*An administrative region or division; adjectivally it describes people of the right type who live in the country*
KIZE	*A* TINE *in the Isle of Wight, renowned for its* YOTTIN *and* RIGGEARTAH
K'N-FINDID	*An adjective expressing restrained exasperation*

KINETEH

An administrative region or division; adjectivally it describes people of the right type who live in the country

———◆———

KOSS-WORLDS	*A range of hills in* **GLAWST-SHAH**
KRAIR	*A country in Asia*
KRAIRNS	*Natives of* **KRAIR**
KRIGGIT	*The famous and ancient* **GEM**, *played on a* **GRIND**. *See* **THE AYVAL, ELL-TRAIRF'D** *and* **LODD'S**
KRINE-JOOLS	*See* **JERL-REH**
KUMP'NEH	*A* **COPPRIT** *entity or a body of people*

LAIRNK-SHAH   *A* KINETEH *somewhere* UP NOTH

LARV-LID-SEE-YOUR   *A fairly standard expression of apparent pleasure when meeting an aquaintance*

LAR-BIL'TEH	*A noun meaning obligation or risk as in* LIM'TID LAR-BIL'TEH KUMP'NEH. *It can also be used to describe a person who is not* R'LARBLE
LATHE	*Verb meaning to hate*
LAW-MER	*A machine for cutting grass*
L'CRAWCE	*One of the* GEMZ *played by* GELS *at school*
LERNBEH-HELD	*An expression indicating a surprising revelation or turn of events*
LIBBER-DEH	*Normally used as describing nerve or cheek, as in* BIDDER-VER LIBBER-DEH
L'KYAR	*That which is sometimes drunk after dinner*

LODD'S   *A very famous* KRIGGIT GRIND *in London*

LODGE   *Adjective meaning big. Also a type of small* HICE *where one may stay when* SHOOTIN

LOI'R   *A member of the legal profession; either a* BEARER-STAH *or* SLIZDAH

LUNGE   *What you eat in the middle of the day. See* POTTY *and* MUZD'V-LUNGE

L'CRAWCE

One of the GEMZ played by GELS at school

MAIRN See CHAIRP

'MAIRNDAH *A* GEL's *name*

MAIRNDLAIR *A* TINE *in* BAMA

MAIRNDRUN *Old name for a senior Chinese* GUMMENT *official as well as the official Chinese language, and a well-known* AYTELL *in Hong Kong*

MAITAH	*The name given to one's car as well as one's mother*
MARM-PAR	*The old couple one occasionally goes* DINE *to spend the weekend with*
MAWCH-REH	*A place where dead bodies are kept*
MAWS	*Upland areas where one shoots* GRICE
'MBAIRSTER	*A senior member of the Diplomatic Corps. See* EM'SEH
M'DAHFELLAY	*A mildly affectionate way of addressing another male*
M'DRAWCE	*A* TINE *in* INJURE
MEDSUN	*Stuff you take if you are ill. See* HOLLY STRIT

MED'TRAINYAN	*Sea to the* CITHE *of* YORUP
MEGGINTOSH	*A waterproof* KATE. *See* BURBRUH
MERRIGGER	*The* CONT'NENT *lying between the* P'CIVIC *and* 'TLAIRNTIC ASIANS. *Sometimes known as* NICE-DAYS-MERRIGGER
MIMRAR	*A direction as to the degree of cooking of one's beef*
M'LAIR	*A country in Asia*
M'LAIRN	*Native of* M'LAIR *as well as a* TINE *in* IDD'LEH
M'NGUMMREH	*Well-known Second World War general*

MWAH!

*This is not so much a word, but a sound always
uttered when kissing someone else (compulsory at*
DRINK-SPOTTIES)

M'NULLAH — *The* CAIRPTLE *of the* FILLY-BINS

MOLLBRA — *A public school in* WILT-CHAH

MUZD'V-LUNGE — *An expression meaning that you do not really want to have* LUNGE *with the person to whom you have said it*

MUZGIBBIN-TUDGE — *Similar to the above except that you do not really want to see them again*

MWAH! — *This is not so much a word, but a sound always uttered when kissing someone else (compulsory at* DRINK-SPOTTIES*)*

NAH-IDGEL   *A* CHAIRP*'s name*

NAIRG   *A* CLAIK-YAL *term for a horse*

NESH'NL   *A famous event in the* RACIN *calendar, and a* GAIRY *in London*

NEVVEH   *See* ROLL NEVVEH

NEWBRUH	*A* RACECOSS *in* BOCKSHAH
NEWMOKKIT	*A* RACECOSS *in* KEMBRIDGE-SHAH
NICE-DAYS-MERRIGGER	*USA*
NISH-TIV	*The sort of thing that* CHAIRPS *ought to show if they want to get anywhere*
NOOVAY	*A convenient way of describing someone who tries hard to be, but isn't*
NORN ARLAND	*Part of the island of* ARLAND. *Most people only go there if they are* PASTED *there by the* OMMEH
NOTH	OP-SIT *of* CITHE
'NSHAWNCE	*A means of protection against loss*
'NTAINYAH	*A* GEL's *name*

NAH-IDGEL

A CHAIRP's *name*

OMMEH   *The second of HM's services*

OP'RAH   *Dramatic musical performance*

OP-SIT   *Converse or corresponding*

ORF	*The OP-SIT of on*
ORFEN	*Frequently*
ORLER-BEST	*An expression of good will, sometimes uttered when having a drink*
ORNREH	*An adjective indicating normality; the OP-SIT of STRORNREH*

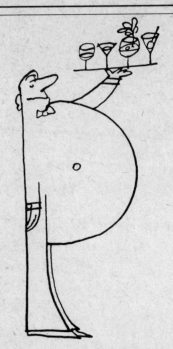

PAINIES   *Small horses. See*
                PAYLAY

PAIRNMAR   *A type of* **HAIRT**

PARLS   *See* **JERL-REH**

PASTED   *Having been sent
                somewhere abroad on
                official business*

PAYLAY	A GEM played on PAINIES
P'CIVIC	The largest ASIAN, to the west of MERRIGGER
PELL MELL	A famous row of CLARBS in SN'JEMZIZ
PERT-TREH	Verse; the last resort if the FLAHZ fail to win the GEL
PHEDDIZ	A public school in Scotland
PIGGERDILLAIR	A well-known London thoroughfare
PINED	A unit of Sterling currency, equivalent to 100p
PINE-DER-BIDDER	A glass of beer

P'LIDDIGLE   *Appertaining to* POL-
             TIX. *See* POTTY

PLOZZER   *A public square or place,*
             and sometimes an
             AYTELL

POGGIT   *A small sack or cavity*
             inserted in CLAITHES
             for carrying things. See
             HAIRNGAJIFF

POIN DER POINT   *This is a type of* RACIN
                  where the actual business
                  of watching the creatures
                  running ABITE *is of no*
                  significance whatever.
                  The whole purpose of a
                  POIN DER POINT *is to*
                  be seen opening the right
                  type of car boot, taking
                  out the right type of
                  hamper and talking to the
                  right type of people

PASTED

Having been sent somewhere abroad on official business

HOT SOJURN

A type of doctor often found in HOLLY STRIT

POL-TIX	*The* SARNCE *and art of* GUMMENT
PORCH-AGLE	*A country in* YORUP
POTT	*A type of fortified red* WAH-IN, *usually drunk after dinner*
POTTRICH	*A bird for* SHOOTIN *and then eating*
POTTY	*A* SAYSHLE *gathering as in* DRINK-SPOTTY, HIGH-SPOTTY, GODDEN POTTY *or* LUNGE POTTY. *It also means a group as in* P'LIDDIGLE POTTY
PRAIK-YAL	*Appertaining to a parish; narrow, provincial*
PRAY-PRIT	*Fit or suitable*
PREFFICE	*An introductory statement*

PROBLIM   *A dilemma*

PROO   *Country in* CITHE
                 MERRIGGER, *as well as
                 a* GEL's *name*

PROP'LEH   *Really or correctly*

PUBLIC HICE   *See* WART'RN-HELL

P'YAHS   *A* CHAIRP's *name quite
                 commonly encountered at*
                 DRINK-SPOTTIES.
                 Others include
                 CHOLLS, EARNDROO,
                 GERMY, HAIRY,
                 H'YOOGAY, JAH-ILLS,
                 NAH-IDGEL,
                 ROO-PUT, *and*
                 YEARN. *Among the*
                 GELS, *one might well
                 bump into:* CARE-LINE,
                 CAT-TRAINER,
                 C'MELLAH,
                 JOOLYAH,
                 'MAIRNDAH,
                 'NTAINYAH, PROO,
                 and SURRAH

ORLER-BEST

An expression of good will, sometimes uttered when having a drink

RACECOSS   *A place where* RACIN *happens, e.g.* NEWBRUH, NEWMOKKIT, *and* SANDINE

RACIN   *The business of watching the* NAIRGS *and possibly owning and/or training them as well*

RAING	*The present participle of the verb 'to row'*
RAIRMBLAHS	*A* KRIGGIT CLARB *for which* ELDY TAINYANS *play*
RARTS	*Occasions when the people get a bit agitated*
RAVER	*A solid type of* BRIDDESH MAITAH
RAY-JAY	*The popular word for* WAHLISS
RER-AL	*Appertaining to the country;* OP-SIT *of* UBBAN
RETARD	*No longer doing one's daily work*
RIGGEARTAH	*An event at e.g.* KIZE *or* HENLAIR

RIND	*One's turn to buy the drinks at a* WART'RN-HELL, PUBLIC HICE, CLARB, *etc. The conversation might run approximately as follows:* 'SMY RIND, WAD'YA-GENNER-HAIRV?' 'JEAN-TEA.' 'HARBOUR-CHEW, PINE-DER-BIDDER?' 'D'MYNIFFER-DOO.' 'WISKIN-SADER?' 'VEDDEH DIZZEN-VIEW, ELL-MAIRN.' 'SEMMER-GEN?' 'CHURZ.' 'ORLER-BEST.'
R'LARBLE	*Solid or dependable*
ROLL EARFOSS	*The junior service*
ROLL NEVVEH	*The senior service*
ROO-PUT	*A* CHAIRP's *name*

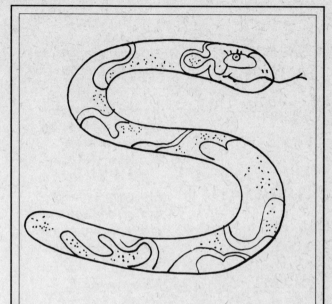

SABER	*Restrained; not intoxicated*
SAFER	*A long piece of FUNNY-CHAH for sitting on*
SAIVY CHOONION	*The world's largest country*
SANDINE	*A famous RACECOSS in Surrey*

SARNCE	*The state or fact of knowledge;* OP-SIT *of art*
SAYSHLE	*Someone who knows the right kind of people, and who goes to lots of* POTTIES
SAYSHLIST	*Unsavoury, left-wing type, nothing whatever to do with, in fact, quite the* OP-SIT *of,* SAYSHLE
SCOFF	*Neckwear (plural* SCOVS*). See* CR'VAIRT
SELL-JAH	*A* MAIRN *in the* OMMEH
SEMMER-GEN	*A repeat of what one was drinking hitherto*
SEMPLEH	*An adjective of great emphasis. See* GOSSLEH

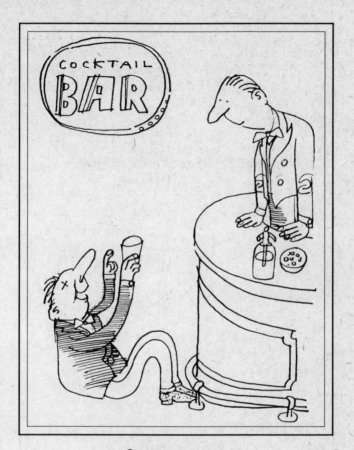

SEMMER-GEN

A repeat of what one was drinking hitherto

SHEDDEH	A type of fortified WAH-IN grown in the region of Jerez
SHOOTIN	Present participle of the verb 'to shoot'
SHRAISEBREH	A public school in Shropshire
SHRAIVE CHOOZDY	The eve of Lent
SHUT	Part of one's WAR-DRABE worn on the torso, but seldom anything but stripes or checks
SIDDEH, THE	London EC
SLAIN	Not only an area of Chelsea, but an adjective describing a whole ethos and syndrome of characteristics exhibited by people who might be unable to understand the relevance to them of this book

SQUIZZIT

Consummate; delightful

SLIZDAH   *A type of* LOI'R

SLON   *An island to the* CITHE
                 of INJURE *whose*
                 CAIRPTLE *is*
                 CLUMBAY

SMAKIN   *The present participle of*
                 the verb 'to smoke'; see
                 also JAIRKIT *and*
                 WAR-DRABE

SNAWT   *See* SNIPH-TAH

SNIPH-TAH   *A quick drink, usually a*
                 WISKIN-SADER, *a*
                 glass of SHEDDEH *or a*
                 JEAN-TEA; *roughly the*
                 same as a SNAWT

SN'JEMZIZ   *An area of London,*
                 famous for its CLARBS,
                 Palace and Court

SN'MOGGRITS   *Well-known* CHUTCH
                 in Westminster

SPAH	*The tapering portion of the steeple of a* CHUTCH *(as opposed to a* TAH*)*
SPOT-SKATE	*See* JAIRKIT
SQUIZZIT	*Consummate; delightful*
SQUORSH	*A* GEM *played between two people on an indoor court*
STAY	*A public school in* BUCK'NM-SHAH
STCHOPPID	*Term of mild abuse, alleging stupidity, as in* DERBISSER STCHOPPID
STERN THE WORLD	*A* TINE *in* GLAWST-SHAH
STIRS	*The things you walk up to get to the next floor*

STRAIRND	*A street leading westwards from* THE SIDDEH
STRERLYAH	*Antipodean ex-colony*
STRERLYAN	*A famous* PUBLIC HICE *in London*
STRORNREH	*An adjective indicating extreme abnormality; the* OP-SIT *of* ORNREH
SURRAH	*A* GEL's *name*

VERCAIRBREH

One's repertoire of words

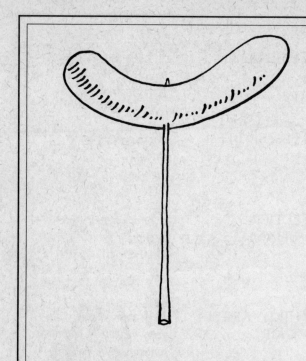

TAH	*See* SPAH; *also see* JERL-REH
TARSUM	*Irritating or mildly infuriating*
TAYKYAY	*The* CAIRPTLE *of* CHPAIRN

TEARLIANS	*A Latin race,* *natives of* IDD'LEH
TEDDER-BLEH	*An adverb meaning* *extremely, awfully,* *frightfully or* VEDDEH
TEDDER- **BLINNICE**	*A complimentary* *description as in* 'SHEZA TEDDER-BLINNICE GEL'
THIRDYARZER- **GAIR**	*Very approximately 30* *years previously, although* *sometimes still meaning* FAWTHWAW
THLEDDIX	*The sort of thing one used* *to do at the Prep*
TIGGIT	*A voucher or card for* *admission to premises*

TINE	*The* CAIRPTLE *of England, to which one always goes* UP *(although this use of the word has genteel overtones). Also means a large built-up settlement*
'TLAIRNTIC	*The* ASIAN *between* MERRIGGER *and* YORUP
TOOTH-IZIN GINNEARS	*A famous horse-race held at* NEWMOKKIT
TOUGH-CLARB	*The governing body of the* RACIN *fraternity*
TRELBEH	*A type of* HAIRT *one wears* RACIN
TRYZERS	*Part of one's* WAR-DRABE, *worn on the legs*
TWIGGERS	*The mecca of Rugby Union*

VUBBLE-DAR-RARE

An illness prevalent at DRINK-SPOTTIES

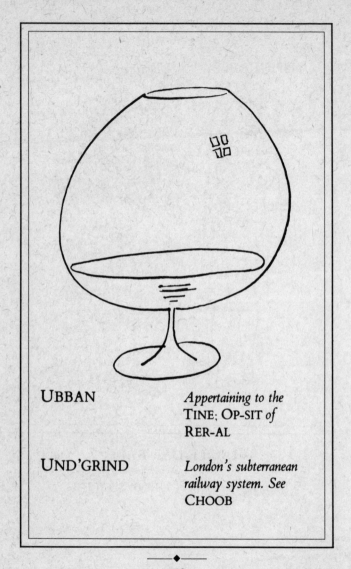

UBBAN

Appertaining to the TINE; OP-SIT *of* RER-AL

UND'GRIND

London's subterranean railway system. See CHOOB

UNSPIGGABLE   *Unmentionable*

UP   OP-SIT *of* DINE; *always used when describing a journey to London (from whatever direction) and when describing attendance at the* VOSSTEH

URNLEH   *Sole or single*

VAIR *See* VEDDEH

VALDY-ZAIR *This is the right sort of place to be seen on a skiing holiday – or, rather, it used to be, since rumour has it that its* SAYSHLE *standing is on the decline. Suitable alternatives are* VARBYAY *and* ZUMMATT

VAR-CHEW	*Goodness or inherent merit*
VARDUCT	*An elevated structure for carrying a railway. See* HAYB'N
VARLENCE	*The sort of thing one really ought to condemn*
VEDDEH	*Extremely; this word is so pronounced when used emphatically. It can also be pronounced* VAIR, *as in* 'THANK YOU VAIR MUCH'
VEE-NAY	*Any type of table* WAH-IN
VERCAIRBREH	*One's repertoire of words*
VOSSTEH	*Oxford and* KEM-BRIDGE *Universities*
V'RARTEH	*Type or diversity*
VUBBLE-DAR-RARE	*An illness prevalent at* DRINK-SPOTTIES

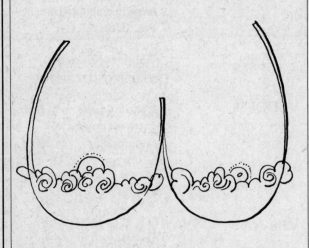

WAD'YA-GENNER-HAIRV? *An enquiry as to what the addressee would like to drink. See* RIND

WAH-IN *The fermented juice of the grape*

WAHLISS *The proper term for* RAY-JAY

WAR-DRABE   *A collection of a*
CHAIRP's CLAITHES
as well as the place in which
he keeps the same, consisting
of, e.g., CR'VAIRTS,
HAIRTS (BAILERS,
BAITERS, PAIRNMARS *and*
TRELBEHS), JUZZEHS,
SCOVS, SHUTS, SMAKIN
JAIRKITS, SPOT-
SKATES, TRYZERS
and WESSKITS

WART'RN-HELL   *The name used to describe*
the right sort of PUBLIC
HIZES, *often found in the*
SW1 area, such as the
AMRAL COD, *the*
ANDERLAPE, *the*
JUKER BOOT *and the*
STRERLYAN. *It is important*
to be in work uniform –
even better, in tails – and to
stand ABITE *– outside in*
the road in good weather –
and make a great deal
of noise

WATCH-UDOUR

A standard opening to a DRINK-SPOTTY *conversation, being in fact an enquiry as to one's job; the answer is often met with* AIR-RALLY, *or nothing at all (since the enquirer's attention has been diverted)*

WESSKIT

Part of a suit, worn between the SHUT *and the* KATE, *and above the* TRYZERS

WESS'N SMER

An island in the P'CIVIC ASIAN

WHINGE-STAH

An historic city in HAIRNTS, *famous for its college*

WHY

49th member of NICE-DAYS-MERRIGGER, *also an island in the* P'CIVIC ASIAN

WISKIN-SADER

A popular drink, consisting of soda water and some Scotch

WILT-CHAH | *A* KINETEH *to the west of London*

WIMMEL-D'N | *The mecca of tennis*

WISKIN-SADER | *A popular drink, consisting of soda water and some Scotch*

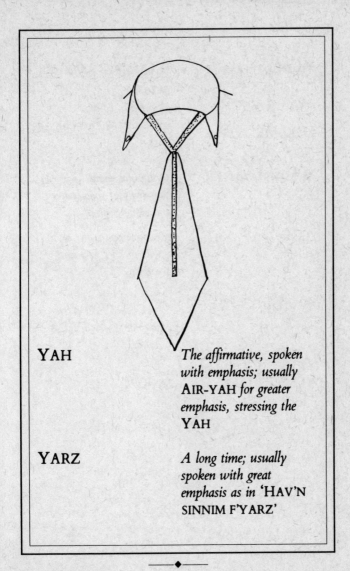

YAH
The affirmative, spoken with emphasis; usually AIR-YAH *for greater emphasis, stressing the* YAH

YARZ
A long time; usually spoken with great emphasis as in 'HAV'N SINNIM F'YARZ'

YEARN	*A CHAIRP's name*
YOB-RAH	*A hand of cards, containing no card above a nine*
YOCKSHAH	*A KINETEH in the NOTH of England*
YOO-NAY	*An inconsequential and vague interjection, mid-sentence*
YORUP	*The CONT'NENT the other side of the English Channel*
YOTTIN	*See KIZE*

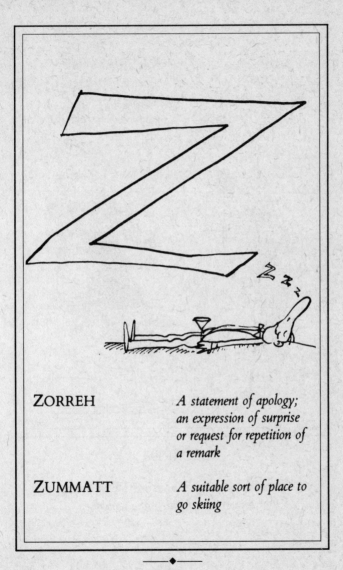

ZORREH

A statement of apology; an expression of surprise or request for repetition of a remark

ZUMMATT

A suitable sort of place to go skiing

ZORREH

A statement of apology; an expression of surprise or request for repetition of a remark

GOLDEN RULES
FOR DRINK-SPOTTIES

ALWAYS
arrive at least HAR PHNAR late

ALWAYS
make a lot of noise, at all times but especially when leaving

ALWAYS
kiss every GEL, on both sides of the face

ALWAYS
say MWAH! with great emphasis when doing so

ALWAYS
tell every GEL that it's LARV LID see her

NEVER
enunciate a person's name when effecting an introduction

NEVER
remember the name of the person to whom you've just
been introduced

ALWAYS
say to every GEL when you kiss goodbye
that you MUZD'V-LUNGE with her or that you
MUZGIBBIN-TUDGE, or both